WORLD WAR II

WEAPONS OF WORLD WAR II

Mike Taylor

**Visit us at
www.abdopub.com**

Published by Abdo Publishing Company, 4940 Viking Drive, Edina, MN 55435.
Copyright ©1998 by Abdo Consulting Group, Inc. International copyrights reserved
in all countries. No part of this book may be reproduced in any form without written
permission from the publisher.

Printed in the United States.

Graphic Design: John Hamilton
Contributing Editors: Alan Gergen; John Hamilton; Morgan Hughes
Cover photo: Digital Stock
Interior photos: AP/Wide World Photos, page 22
　　　　　　　　Digital Stock, pages 1, 3, 4, 6, 10, 13, 14, 17, 18, 19, 20, 21, 23, 27

Sources: Boyne, Walter J. *Clash of Wings: World War II in the Air.* New York:
Simon & Schuster, 1997; Boyne, Walter J. *Clash of Titans: World War II At Sea.*
New York: Simon & Schuster, 1994; Churchill, Winston S. *The Second World War.*
6 vols., New York, 1948-1953; Stokesbury, James. *A Short History of World War II.*
New York: William Morrow and Company, 1980; Weinberg, Gerhard. *A World At
Arms, A Global History of World War II.* Cambridge University Press, 1994; Wright,
Gordon. *The Ordeal of Total War, 1939-1945.* New York: Harper and Row, 1968.

Library of Congress Cataloging–in–Publication Data

Taylor, Mike.
　　Weapons of World War II / Mike Taylor
　　　　p. cm. — (World War II)
　　Includes index.
　　Summary: Describes some of the weapons used by both the Allied and Axis
forces during World War II, including automatic weapons, radar, early
computers, tanks, aircraft carriers, bombers and fighter planes, and the atomic
bomb.
　　ISBN　1-56239-808-3
　　1. Military weapons—History—20th century—Juvenile literature. 2. World
War, 1939-1945—equipment and supplies—Juvenile literature.　[1. World War,
1939-1945—equipment and supplies. 2. Military weapons.] I. Title. II. Series:
World War II　(Edina, Minn.)
UF500.T38　1998
623.4' 09' 044—dc21　　　　　　　　　　　　　　97-46510
　　　　　　　　　　　　　　　　　　　　　　　　CIP
　　　　　　　　　　　　　　　　　　　　　　　　AC

CONTENTS

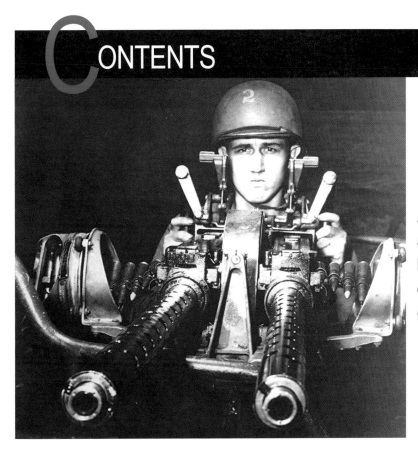

A sailor aboard a U.S. Navy PT boat aims a .50-caliber machine gun.

WEAPONS OLD AND NEW

The largest war in history, World War II, was fought between 1939 and 1945. In World War II the Allies, led by Great Britain, the United States, and the Soviet Union, were able to defeat the Axis powers, led by Germany, Japan, and Italy, with tremendous new weapons. There were huge new aircraft carriers and "Flying Fortress" bombers. There were tanks and tiny new boats called landing craft.

Sixteen-inch guns of the battleship USS *Iowa*.

New technology, like radio and radar, was also very important in World War II. Finally, most destructive of all was the atomic bomb. This book explains how some of the new weapons were used by the Allies and the Axis powers.

World War II began in 1939, when Germany invaded Poland. The Battle of Poland demonstrates the mixture of old and new weapons used in World War II. The Germans invaded with high-speed armored tanks and powerful fighter aircraft. The Poles were not prepared for war. They did not have modern weapons and tried heroically to defend their country with cavalry (horses) and swords.

The Battle of Poland lasted only two weeks before the Poles were defeated. The Germans captured almost the entire Polish army. Poland became a part of the German empire.

Germany's ally, Japan, used powerful new weapons as well. With new navy ships and airplanes, Japan was able to conquer most of the islands in the South Pacific during 1939. Japan's superior weapons made possible its surprise attack on Pearl Harbor, on the Hawaiian island of Oahu, in 1941.

The victories of the Axis powers frightened the leaders of the other countries. The Allies responded by quickly modernizing their own weapons to match those of their enemies. Great Britain, the Soviet Union, and the United States developed powerful weapons of their own. In the end, all kinds of weapons, small and large, were needed in order to defeat Germany and Japan, and to ensure victory for the Allies.

RIFLES AND MACHINE GUNS

A Marine draws a bead on a Japanese sniper.

Some weapons were not so new at all. The most important weapon was still the trusty rifle. Soldiers in World War I (1914-1918) used rifles that were as good as those used by any army in World War II. In World War I the rifles worked very well because the fighting took place in open fields and demanded long, accurate shots. The armies, therefore, developed rifles to fire such shots. These rifles were still in use by many armies in World War II. Even brand new rifles were not much different from the old ones used in World War I.

By World War II, however, all armies began to make more use of guns that automatically reloaded themselves. These automatic weapons, also called "machine guns," were less accurate, and could not shoot as far. However, machine guns were more useful in the new style of fighting because they could shoot more quickly. Many battles were fought in cities from building to building, house to house, and did not demand long, accurate shots. Quick shots worked much better. One soldier with a machine gun could defend a whole street against several enemy soldiers armed with old rifles.

For example, during the winter of 1942-1943, Germany and the Soviet Union fought a great battle in the Soviet city of Stalingrad. The German and Soviet soldiers fought street-to-street and building-to-building for many months. They needed compact weapons that they could carry easily and shoot quickly from doors and windows.

Because the machine guns fired so quickly, they used a tremendous amount of ammunition. Gradually, the Germans in Stalingrad began to run out of ammunition. By January 1943, the Germans had run out of food as well. The German leader, Adolf Hitler, would not allow his men to surrender, but ordered them instead to fight to the end. By February, the Soviet army had surrounded the Germans inside a few square blocks within the city of Stalingrad. German machine guns were quiet, and the starving German soldiers finally surrendered.

This new style of warfare, with the use of machine guns, was very brutal. Germany began the battle of Stalingrad with 300,000 men. By February 1943, when they surrendered, there were 91,000 still alive. The Soviets lost between 225,000 and 300,000 soldiers.

CODE BREAKING AND SPIES

Espionage, or spying, also was used in World War I. It was much more important, however, in World War II. The new kinds of espionage were even more important. Radio espionage, for example, meant secretly intercepting the radio messages of enemies. Soldiers spoke only in code when they spoke by radio and hoped that the enemy would not understand the code. The spy's job was to learn the enemy's code and decode the messages into plain language. Specialists used sophisticated radio equipment to intercept the messages. Then the intercepted message was given to more specialists (called "cryptologists") for decoding. The world's first computers were invented by specialists during World War II in order to decode messages.

Radio espionage altered the course of the war. In 1941, an Italian spy stole a top-secret American code book from an American officer in Rome. The Italian spy gave the American code book to the Germans, who made good use of it in their radio espionage. Because the Americans did not know of the loss, they did not change their code. The Germans were able to understand the radio messages between their American and British enemies.

This gave the Germans a great advantage in the Battle of the Atlantic, from 1940 to 1942. British ships needed to cross the Atlantic Ocean from America to Great Britain. They carried food for the British people and military supplies for the British army. The German navy, with its dangerous submarine "U-boats," decoded the radio messages between enemy British ship captains. From these messages the Germans learned the locations of the British ships. The German U-boats were able to attack British ships successfully. These German attacks made it very difficult for Allied ships to cross the Atlantic Ocean from America to Great Britain. This caused major shortages in Great Britain. The people often did not have enough to eat. The army often lacked supplies. The Germans hoped that the hungry British people and army would give up quickly.

By the spring of 1943, British spies had turned the tables and broken the German codes and could listen to German radio messages. This helped British ships to avoid the German U-boats and to carry more supplies to Great Britain. The Germans could not prevent ships from carrying supplies to Great Britain. Food and supplies actually became more abundant in Great Britain and more scarce in Germany. The Allies eventually won the important Battle of the Atlantic because of their successful radio espionage.

The new spies helped the Allies in other battles as well. In the Pacific Ocean the American navy used radio espionage to intercept so many conversations among the enemy Japanese that they quickly broke the Japanese secret code. This allowed the United States to know many of Japan's most secret plans.

Radio espionage did not help to prevent the successful Japanese attack on Pearl Harbor in Hawaii on December 7, 1941, because the Japanese used strict radio silence. They did not use their radios at all so that American listeners could not hear them. Because the Japanese ships silenced their radios, the Americans had no way of knowing the Japanese were coming, and they could not prepare to defend themselves. Japanese radio silence ensured that the attack would be a complete surprise. Much of the American fleet was destroyed by the Japanese surprise attack on Pearl Harbor, and it took many months before the sunken ships could be replaced.

The USS *Shaw* explodes during the Japanese raid on Pearl Harbor.

After the attack on Pearl Harbor, the Americans quickly improved their espionage. It helped the United States and Great Britain to turn the war in the Pacific Ocean back in their favor.

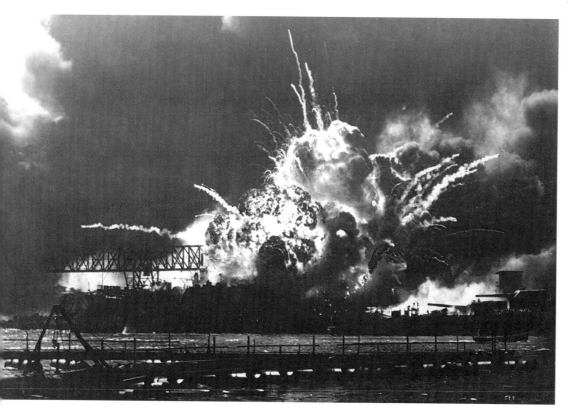

RADAR

Radar was one of the most important inventions of the World War II era. Radar sends a radio signal out to a target. The signal bounces off and returns to the radar unit. By measuring the time it takes for the signal to bounce off the target and return, radar operators can measure the distance to a target.

With radar, ships could more easily locate enemy vessels. They could even measure how fast those ships were moving and in what direction. Radar was very important in submarines, which spent most of their time under water. They did not even have windows. Radar was the only way they could know when other ships were near them on the ocean's surface.

Radar was also very important in air warfare. Indeed, the British invented radar in order to help defend their coastline against enemy airplanes. In 1940, very early in the war, the British installed radar units along the coast of Great Britain.

These radar units were invaluable during the famous Battle of Britain in August and September of 1941. This was the greatest air battle of the whole war. British radar prevented surprise attacks from the enemy air force, the German Luftwaffe. When British radar detected approaching German planes, their pilots "scrambled." They ran to their own fighter aircraft and took off very quickly. They often intercepted the German bombers over the English Channel before they could drop any bombs on British soil.

BLITZKRIEG AND TANK WARFARE

A tank is a military vehicle that drives on tracks, so that it cannot become stuck easily. It has a large cannon and a smaller machine gun. Tanks are covered with steel armor so they cannot be destroyed by any but the largest explosion.

A few tanks had been used in World War I, but they were not very helpful. In the European battles of World War II, however, tanks played a very important role.

During the first half of World War II, it was the Germans who made best use of their tanks. The best German tanks were the famous Mark IV tanks. They were mid-sized and very fast.

The Germans used the Mark IV tanks in *Blitzkrieg* fashion, or "lightning warfare." *Blitzkrieg* meant that the tanks would speed out in front, covered by fighter airplanes directly above. The *Blitzkrieg* would quickly punch a hole through the enemy lines. Then the regular foot soldiers could march through more easily and more quickly.

The German *Blitzkrieg* worked very well during the first years of the war. However, by 1943 the Soviet Union had developed the great T-34 tank. Its protective armor was very thick, and its cannon could make very long shots. The Soviet T-34 was more than a match for the German Mark IV.

The United States also developed mid-sized tanks: the famous Sherman tanks. These were even smaller than the German Mark IV's. But the Shermans were very reliable, and the American army had enough of them to outnumber the German tanks in most battles.

The Germans developed new, larger-sized tanks, the Panther and the Tiger. They hoped these huge new tanks could overpower the smaller Soviet T-34's and American Shermans.

In the summer of 1943, the largest tank battle in history was fought at the city of Kursk in the Soviet Union. The Germans attacked with 2,500 Panthers and Tigers and 900,000 men. But the new German tanks were *too* big! They were slow and could not turn quickly. The smaller and quicker T-34's surrounded the German tanks. The heavy German tanks often sank in the mud. A stuck tank was an easy target. A single soldier could climb onto the tank and drop a hand grenade inside it.

The Soviet Union won the great tank battle of Kursk in 1943. The German army lost many of its tanks in the battle. The successes of the smaller Soviet T-34's and American Sherman tanks proved that bigger is not always better.

Protected by a Sherman tank, U.S. troops of the 60th Infantry advance into Belgium.

NEW SHIPS IN NAVAL WARFARE

An aircraft carrier task force cruises toward the Philippines.

Most of the kinds of ships used in World War II were not very new. Battleships and destroyers had both been used in World War I. Even submarines had been used in World War I. The two types of ships that were brand new in World War II were the great aircraft carriers and the tiny landing craft. These were the largest and the smallest ships in the war. Each was important in its own way.

An aircraft carrier (also called a "flat top") is a floating airport. It is large enough to carry many airplanes, and has a runway where the airplanes can land and take off. In World War II, aircraft carriers were as long as a football field. They were constructed by thousands of engineers, welders, and technicians in special factories near the ocean. Usually one or more aircraft carriers would escort a group of battleships and destroyers as they crossed the ocean. The planes could be used to defend the ships or attack the enemy fleet.

The aircraft carriers of World War II changed naval warfare drastically. The planes could fly far from their base to seek out and bomb the enemy fleet. In this way, air battles could be fought thousands of miles from land. Even the fighting aircraft carriers might be hundreds of miles apart, their airplanes buzzing overhead.

This was the case in the great Battle of the Coral Sea in May, 1942. American planes from the aircraft carriers *Lexington* and *Yorktown* ambushed a Japanese fleet in the Coral Sea on May 2, 1942. By the end of the battle, four days later, the American planes sank two Japanese aircraft carriers and two destroyers. Japanese planes so badly damaged one American aircraft carrier, the *Lexington*, it had to be scuttled. All of this was done without the Japanese and American ships ever coming within sight of each other.

Aircraft carriers were also very important in the Battle of Midway in June, 1942. Midway is a small group of islands owned by the United States. The islands are located in the center of the Pacific Ocean. The Japanese hoped to capture the islands, and sent a fleet of more than 200 ships, with four heavy aircraft carriers. The American navy defended Midway with a large fleet and three aircraft carriers. One of the American carriers was the *Yorktown*, which was damaged, but not sunk, at the Battle of the Coral Sea.

The Battle of Midway was a tremendous victory for the United States. Planes launched from carriers sank all four of the Japanese heavy aircraft carriers and many other ships also. The *Yorktown* did not survive the battle. Japanese planes heavily bombed the carrier and a Japanese submarine torpedo finally sank it.

Although the landing craft of World War II was tiny compared to the mighty aircraft carrier, it was just as important. Most of the ships used in World War II were so large that they could dock only in very large harbors. When commanders wanted to attack islands or beaches away from the harbors, they used small boats to move soldiers from the large ships to the shore. These small boats were called landing craft.

After the Battle of Midway, the American navy hoped to capture other islands in the South Pacific from the Japanese. They used hundreds of landing craft to transport their soldiers ashore. The small boats loaded with men were moved right up to the shore. Then the front end folded down like a ramp. The soldiers then poured out onto the beach. In the meanwhile, the larger ships stayed far out at sea. Landing craft were used in this way in the most famous battles of the Pacific Ocean, including the battles of Guadalcanal and Iwo Jima.

The largest use of landing craft was in the great invasion of Normandy, France, on "D-Day," June 6, 1944. The D-Day invasion was the largest single attack in the war. Great Britain and the United States hoped to attack at Normandy and push the Germans out of France. The Allies gathered nearly three million troops and thousands of ships for the invasion.

American soldiers land on the coast of Normandy, France, on D-Day.

On June 6, the weather was very bad and the sea was very rough. The largest ships remained anchored far out to sea. Over 2,500 landing craft transported the soldiers to shore. Because of the high waves, many became seasick aboard the tiny landing craft.

As the 78,000 American and British soldiers stepped out onto shore, the Germans fired down on them from the hillsides. Nearly 5,000 Allied soldiers were killed during the first hours.

Gradually, the landing craft transported enough men and guns so that the soldiers could defend themselves. Then they began to attack the German forces. The D-Day invasion was a great success for the Allies. Within months the Allies had freed Paris and western France from German domination. Soon the Allies would push the Germans out of France completely.

Although the landing craft were much smaller than the aircraft carrier, they were very important in World War II. It is hard to imagine how the Allies could have won the war without the invention of this small boat.

1939 *September:* Battle of Poland. German *Blitzkrieg* overwhelms Poland with high-speed tanks and aircraft. The Battle of Poland is the beginning of World War II.

1940 *August and September:* Battle of Britain. Britain uses newly invented radar units and fighter airplanes to intercept German bombers. The Battle of Britain is the largest air battle in World War II.

1940-1943 Battle of the Atlantic. German "U-boats" try to sink British ships transporting supplies to Great Britain. The British use radio espionage to intercept messages from German captains. Specialists invent computers to decode the messages. Radio espionage helps the British to win the Battle of the Atlantic.

1941 *December 7:* Surprise attack on Pearl Harbor. Japanese aircraft carriers stage successful surprise attack and destroy much of the American fleet at Pearl Harbor in Hawaii. Because the Japanese used strict radio silence, it is impossible for the Americans to intercept messages and predict the attack.

1942 Manhattan Project. The United States begins to build an atomic bomb.

1942 *May:* Battle of the Coral Sea. Planes from American and Japanese aircraft carriers fight off the north coast of Australia. The American carrier *Yorktown* is damaged, but not sunk.

1942 *June:* Battle of Midway. One of the greatest battles among aircraft carriers. Japanese aircraft carriers attack, but the Americans are prepared and win the battle decisively. The Americans sink four Japanese aircraft carriers. The Japanese sink one American carrier, the *Yorktown.*

1942-1943 *Winter:* Battle of Stalingrad. Germans and Soviets engage in street-to-street and building-to-building battle for the Soviet city of Stalingrad. Small machine guns are very important to this style of fighting. In February 1943, the Germans run out of ammunition and supplies, and the surviving Germans surrender. Nearly 500,000 Soviet and German troops lose their lives in the battle.

1943 *June:* Battle of Kursk. The Soviet Union defeats Germany in the greatest tank battle in history.

1944-1945 Long-range bombing. British Lancaster bombers attack German cities at night, destroying homes and businesses. Meanwhile, American "Flying Fortresses" equipped with the Norden Bombsight bomb more specific targets like factories, oil refineries, and railways.

1944 *June 6:* D-Day. Allied forces use thousands of small landing craft to attack the beaches of northern France. The Allies land so many soldiers in this way that they soon liberate Paris and push the Germans out of France.

1945 *April 30:* German leader Adolf Hitler commits suicide.

1945 *May 8:* V-E Day. Victory in Europe! The Germans surrender to American General Dwight D. Eisenhower.

1945 *August 6:* Hiroshima. The American bomber "Enola Gay" drops an atomic bomb on the Japanese city of Hiroshima. While 80,000 Japanese civilians are killed outright, 10,000 go missing, and 37,000 are seriously injured.

1945 *August 9:* Nagasaki. The United States drops a second atomic bomb on the Japanese city of Nagasaki, killing 35,000 and injuring 6,000.

1945 *August 14:* Japan surrenders to the Allies after witnessing the terrible destruction in the cities of Hiroshima and Nagasaki.

CANNONS, SHELLS, AND MISSILES

U.S. troops on a captured mammoth 274mm German railroad gun.

A cannon is a large gun, too large to be carried by soldiers. Cannons in World War II often had their own wheels and were pulled by trucks. A cannon fires out a destructive bomb called a shell. In World War II all countries tried to build bigger cannons that could fire larger shells farther and farther.

The Germans, for example, wanted to build a huge cannon, large enough to fire a shell all the way from Germany to London, England (approximately 500 miles (805 km)). The Germans hoped that such a weapon might force the British to surrender. This huge cannon was nicknamed "Dora." Its barrel was as long as a football field, and could fire a shell the size of a small car. Despite its large size, "Dora" could not be aimed well. All of the shells landed in the ocean and missed Great Britain completely.

A missile is a kind of shell that is not launched from a cannon. A missile has its own rocket engine instead. When "Dora" did not work as planned, the

Germans tried to bomb London with missiles. The first German missile was called the V-1. The V-1 could carry a one-ton bomb from Germany to London, and traveled at 350 miles per hour (560 km per hour). This was not very fast. The British could use radar to see the missiles coming. Then fighter planes could intercept the missiles and shoot them down.

The second German missile, called the V-2, was much faster. It could fly 3,000 miles per hour (4,800 km per hour)! British fighter planes could not shoot down the V-2 missiles. Luckily, the V-2 missiles were very unreliable. They often exploded in midair, and almost never hit their targets.

Sometimes German missiles flew off course and landed in Germany! In 1944, a German inspector reported that a missile flew off target and landed in a German barnyard. The inspector reported that the missile killed all of the cows and chickens on the farm.

While German missiles frightened the British people greatly, they did not help the Germans much in the war.

An aircraft spotter in London, England.

BOMBERS AND FIGHTER PLANES

A B-17 Flying Fortress long-range bomber.

One of the most important weapons in World War II was the long-distance bomber. This was a large plane, with four engines, that could carry many bombs over a very long distance.

During the first years of the war the British relied on Lancaster bombers. A Lancaster could carry many bombs deep into German territory and still have enough fuel to return to Great Britain. The Lancasters dropped two types of bombs. They dropped simple explosive bombs to destroy buildings and equipment. They also dropped fire bombs to start large fires that burned everything that did not explode.

The Lancasters flew at night so that German fighter airplanes could not see them and shoot them down. In July 1943, the British attacked the German city of Hamburg with over 700 planes. Much of the city was destroyed by either explosions or fires.

Because the Lancaster bombers flew at night, they often could not find the right target. In the Hamburg raid, for example, they mostly hit people's homes and offices rather than military targets. Most of the people killed in Hamburg were not soldiers at all.

By 1942, the United States Air Force had developed a bomber that made it easier to hit the target. This was the famous B-17 bomber, also called the "Flying Fortress." The Flying Fortress had armor plating, 12 machine guns, and a crew of 6. It also had a special tool, the "Norden Bombsight," for aiming its bombs better.

Because the Flying Fortress was more accurate, it was used to bomb the most important military targets, like railways, factories, and oil refineries. The British Lancaster was still used in night missions to bomb cities, where accuracy was not as important.

As the Flying Fortresses flew farther and farther into German territory, they were often shot down by Germany's high-speed fighter planes. The Americans and British had fighter planes, too. However, they could not carry enough fuel to fly with the bombers all the way to their German targets. The fighters would fly with the bombers part of the way, then return to

Soldiers manning an anti-aircraft battery watch planes dogfighting in the skies of Germany.

Britain to refuel. When the Allied fighters turned around, the German fighters attacked the bombers.

In 1943, the United States Air Force began using two new fighter planes to defend their Flying Fortresses. The new Mustang and Thunderbolt fighters had extra fuel tanks mounted on their bellies so that they could fly much farther. When the belly tank was empty, the pilot released it, and it fell to the ground. The pilot switched to fuel tanks in the wings and the fighter continued to defend the larger bombers.

Because the Mustangs and Thunderbolts could now escort so much farther, German fighter planes could no longer shoot down the Flying Fortresses easily. In 1944 and 1945, the American fighters escorted Flying Fortresses on many successful bombing missions deep into German territory.

The British and American bombers destroyed many factories, railways, and oil refineries. The Germans could no longer build new planes. They no longer had enough fuel to fly their existing planes. The success of the long-range bombers and fighter airplanes helped the Allies to defeat Germany.

A P-51 Mustang fighter airplane.

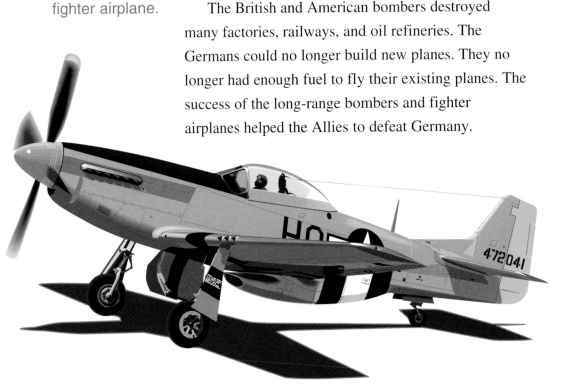

THE ATOMIC BOMB

By far the most powerful and destructive weapon used in World War II was the atomic bomb. The atomic bomb was developed by scientists studying the atoms in uranium, a kind of metal.

During the 1930s, German scientists learned that when a single atom of uranium was split, it released a very large amount of energy. Some German scientists speculated that uranium could be used to make a huge bomb, an atomic bomb. Nobody paid much attention at first because the idea seemed crazy. The German government, however, continued to study the problem, hoping to build an atomic bomb.

In 1939, the famous German scientist Albert Einstein wrote a letter to the American president, Franklin Roosevelt. Einstein, who fled Germany, warned Roosevelt that Germany was working on an atomic bomb. Einstein promised that the idea would work and that the energy could be used for defensive purposes. He urged the United States to build an atomic bomb before the Germans completed their own. The Germans and the Americans raced to construct the first new atomic weapon.

In 1942, President Roosevelt approved a plan to develop an atomic bomb. The plan's code name was the Manhattan Project. Many German scientists who had escaped from Germany now joined the Americans.

Meanwhile, the German effort made little progress. Many of Germany's most expert scientists were forced to flee Germany because they were Jewish. The German government, led by Adolf Hitler, believed that Jewish people were inferior, and persecuted them brutally. The Jewish scientists repaid Hitler by helping the United States with the Manhattan Project.

Splitting uranium atoms causes tremendous heat. It was necessary to cool the scientific tools with a special kind of water, called "heavy water." The Germans could manufacture as much "heavy water" as they needed in a special factory. In 1943, the Allies bombed the "heavy water" factory and destroyed it. That successful mission helped to prevent the Germans from making an atomic bomb during the war.

The Manhattan Project in the United States had much greater success. On July 16, 1945, the United States tested its first atomic bomb at Los Alamos, New Mexico. The scientists set up delicate equipment to measure the size of the explosion. The bomb was more powerful than the scientists had predicted. The explosion destroyed all of their delicate equipment and sent a cloud of dust a mile into the atmosphere!

After the Germans surrendered, the United States decided to use the new weapon against Japan. The new American president, Harry S. Truman, hoped the atomic bomb would force Japan to surrender as well.

On August 6, 1945, an American bomber, the *Enola Gay*, dropped an atomic bomb on the Japanese city of Hiroshima. Three days later another bomber dropped a second atomic bomb on the city of Nagasaki. There was great rejoicing in the United States and Great Britain. The bombs had worked, forcing the Japanese to surrender on August 14.

An atomic bomb explodes over the Japanese city of Nagasaki on August 9, 1945.

The destruction in Japan was frightful. When the bombs exploded, the fire was hot enough to burn cement and to melt steel. Windows melted from buildings. The water in the ponds and rivers boiled. In Hiroshima, 80,000 people were killed instantly, some 37,000 were injured immediately, and more than 10,000 were never found. Much of the city was destroyed completely. Many who survived the explosion became very ill. Many died later of radiation poisoning from the atomic explosion.

Even the Allies were frightened by the destruction caused by the new weapon they had used. Many new, more powerful atomic bombs have been built since World War II. However, none have ever been used. This is probably because of the worldwide fear and the memory of Hiroshima and Nagasaki.

CONCLUSION

Many of the new weapons of World War II are still used today, though they have been changed greatly. The trusty rifle is still the most important weapon. The value of the armored tank and large bombers has been proven in many wars since 1945. Technology like radar is now used for non-military purposes, such as airplane navigation. Fishermen can now purchase radar units to locate fish under the water! Atomic technology is still used to make destructive bombs. However, atomic energy has been harnessed to make electricity as well.

INTERNET SITES

A-Bomb WWW Museum
http://www.csi.ad.jp/ABOMB/index.html
This site provides readers with accurate information concerning the impact of the first atomic bomb on Hiroshima, Japan.

Black Pilots Shatter Myths
http://www.af.mil/news/features/features95/f_950216-112_95feb16.html
This site tells of the exploits of the 332nd Fighter Group, the first all-black flying unit known as the Tuskegee Airmen.

United States Holocaust Museum
http://www.ushmm.org/
The official Web site of the U.S. Holocaust Memorial Museum in Washington, D.C.

What Did You Do In The War, Grandma?
http://www.stg.brown.edu/projects/WWII_Women/tocCS.html
An oral history of Rhode Island women during World War II. In this project, 17 students interviewed 36 Rhode Island women who recalled their lives in the years before, during, and after the Second World War.

World War II Commemoration
http://www.grolier.com/wwii/wwii_mainpage.html
To commemorate the 50th anniversary of the end of the war, Grolier Online assembled a terrific collection of World War II historical materials on the Web. Articles taken from *Encyclopedia Americana* tell the story of World War II, including biographies. Also included are combat films, photographs, a World War II history test, and links to many other sites.

These sites are subject to change. Go to your favorite search engine and type in "World War II" for more sites.

Pass It On
World War II buffs: educate readers around the country by passing on information you've learned about World War II. Share your little-known facts and interesting stories. We want to hear from you! To get posted on the ABDO & Daughters website, E-mail us at "History@abdopub.com"

Visit the ABDO & Daughters website at www.abdopub.com

 29

GLOSSARY

Aircraft Carrier: Aircraft carriers were the largest ships by far in any fleet in World War II. They were equipped with runways on which fighter planes and small bombers could land and take off. This allowed for air battles far out into the ocean, like the Battle of the Coral Sea and the Battle of Midway in May and June of 1942.

Allies: The World War II alliance of Great Britain, the United States, the Soviet Union, and several other smaller states united against Germany and Japan.

Atomic bomb: This was a powerful new type of bomb invented in World War II. The atomic bomb used for its explosion the energy released by splitting a uranium atom. It was a very difficult scientific procedure, and the United States was the only country to have an atomic bomb during the war.

Axis powers: The World War II alliance of Germany, Italy, and Japan. Italy played only a minor role among the Axis powers.

Bomber: A large plane that could carry many tons of bombs far into enemy territory. The bombers were so slow that they were easy targets for enemy fighter planes. Eventually the United States developed the mighty Flying Fortress bomber, with several big machine guns and a crew of up to nine men. The Flying Fortresses destroyed many German factories and railways between 1943 and 1945.

Fighter: A small and fast plane with one pilot that could be used to battle other planes in the air. Fighter planes were often used to escort the large and slow bomber planes over enemy territory.

30

Landing Craft: These were small boats used to transport troops from the larger ships up to the beaches during an attack. The landing craft was a small and simple weapon, but very important to the success of the great D-Day invasion on June 6, 1944, which led to the defeat of Germany.

Machine Gun: A small rifle that can fire many shots very quickly. Machine guns were not very accurate at long distances, but were deadly at close range. Machine guns were very important in the new style of close-range fighting of World War II. The famous Battle of Stalingrad in 1942 and 1943 is a good example.

Manhattan Project: This was the code name for the American atomic bomb program. In 1942 the United States began the Manhattan Project with the hope of developing an atomic bomb before Germany. The Manhattan Project was successful, and scientists completed the first atomic bomb in 1945.

Radar: Radar is an electronic tool invented in World War II to measure the location and movement of enemy planes and ships. Radar helped the British air force to defeat the Germans in the Battle of Britain, the greatest air battle in World War II. Radar is now used for peaceful purposes, like tracking storms.

Tank: A tank is a military vehicle that drives on tracks, so that it cannot become stuck easily. It has a large cannon and a smaller machine gun, and is protected by a heavy armored shell.

U-boat: The name for Germany's deadly submarines in World War II. German U-boats were very effective during the Battle of the Atlantic between 1940 and 1942. However, by 1942 the Allies found ways to avoid the U-boats, and the Germans lost the Battle of the Atlantic.

V-2: The code name for Germany's second type of missile in World War II. Because it was rocket-powered, it could fly much faster than the previous V-1. Luckily, it was also much less accurate than the V-1.